Things To Do...

T5-ACR-733

...In The Smokies

Introduction

"That was a lot of fun and we had a great time, but what else is there to do around here?" Have you ever heard this before? You may have even asked it yourself. Variations of this question are repeated a zillion times every year in the Smoky Mountains. The number of responses you're likely to hear are as varied as the question itself.

The Smokies and the Great Smoky Mountains National Park are a major vacation destination. Winter, spring, summer, and fall people flock to these mountains. Some come only for a day or a weekend, others for months at a time. They come to relax, to have fun, to enjoy the views and the cool mountain air. It's a place for children to play and for adults to become children again. There are *lots* of fun activities for everyone to do—trails for hiking and biking, rivers for tubing and rafting, mountains for climbing, and quiet roads that take you somewhere special or nowhere at all.

You can search for hidden gem stones in the streams and explore ancient forests with monstrous trees. Head for the museums to learn about native plants and animals and rocks, or the history of the Cherokee Indians and the southern highlanders native to this land. You can pick wild blueberries, look at colorful leaves and flowers and you may even spot a bear. You can do all these fun things and more. Many cost very little to do and most are free.

In this book you'll find forty-nine different activities. They're fun, they're inexpensive, and they're great for children and adults alike. On each page there's a brief description of the activity, how to get there, when to go, how long you'll stay, what it will cost, and what to bring along. Sometimes a note will give you a special tip or suggest another nearby activity. The appendix includes several sample itineraries. These should spark a few ideas on how you can use this book to plan a great vacation. I've also suggested some places you might want to stay and some of the services you might want to use.

So...what else is there to do around here? Turn the pages and see for yourself.

J.P.
April, 1993

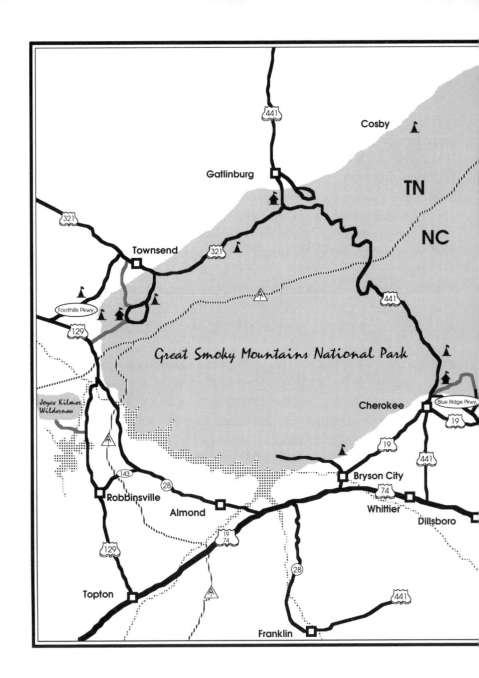

Orientation

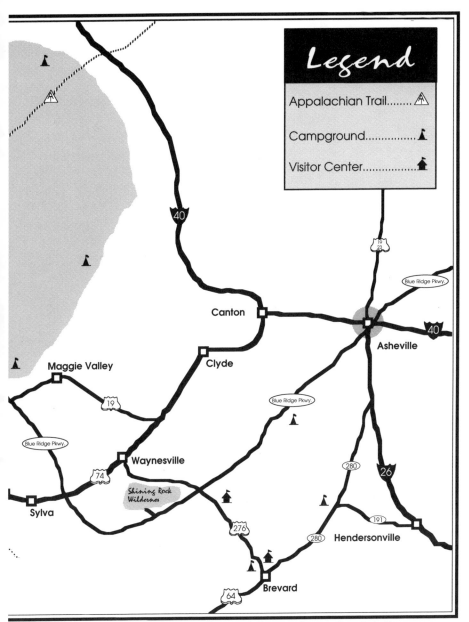

Legend

Appalachian Trail........ ⚠

Campground............... ⛺

Visitor Center............... ⛪

Canton

Asheville

Clyde

Maggie Valley

Waynesville

Sylva

Shining Rock Wilderness

Hendersonville

Brevard

Blue Ridge Pkwy.

Please refer to an atlas or state road map for details.

Map

Museums & Visitor Centers

Sugarlands

This is the headquarters to the Great Smoky Mountains National Park, and the starting point for many visitors. You'll find plenty of information as well as a natural history museum featuring the park's five distinct forest types. Displays feature native animals and plants with a short narrative describing each one, including information on when and where in the park you're likely to spot them. Short, interesting slide shows and presentations occur every half hour or so in a small theatre.

Location
On U.S. 441, just south of Gatlinburg, TN

Season
Year-round

Time Allowance
1 hour

Cost Range
Free admission, although you may want to purchase a book or two in the bookstore.

Bring Along
camera, notepad for recording any information, questions.

Note: Be sure to pick up a free copy of the *Smokies Guide* for up-to-date information on happenings in the Park.

2

Cades Cove

Appalachian pioneer life is the theme of this visitor center. There's even a working grist mill where fresh cornmeal is ground daily. The center is located half way out the one-way Cades Cove Loop Road, and provides a welcome place to stretch your legs while learning more about the families that once settled in this picturesque valley.

Location In the Cable Mill area of Cades Cove, on the Cades Cove Loop Road. This is on the west side of the Park near Townsend, TN.

Season
April - October

Time Allowance
1 - 1.5 hours

Cost Range
Free admission. Fresh-ground cornmeal from the mill can be purchased in the center bookstore.

Bring Along camera, questions.

Note: A trip to this visitor center will always include a tour around the Cades Cove Loop Road (See p. 48). Also, be sure to check at the information desk to see when the next ranger-led walk of the grist mill will occur.

3

Oconaluftee

The southern entrance to the National Park. This center offers an information area, a book store, and a small exhibit space with pictures, artifacts, and narratives focusing on early pioneer life. From the same parking area you can visit the adjacent **Pioneer Farmstead**, a complete working farm. Here you'll find everything from a summer garden to a blacksmith's shop to an outhouse. There's even a pig pen. Kids will enjoy seeing and touching the farm animals that roam freely about.

Location   On U.S. 441, just north of Cherokee, NC

Season
Visitor center: year-round. **Farmstead:** May - October

Time Allowance
1 - 2 hours

Cost Range
Free

Bring Along   camera, notepad for recording any
information, questions, sun protection, something to drink.

Note: The Mingus Mill, a water-powered grist mill just down the road, can make a nice addition to this visit.

4

Museum of the Cherokee Indian

The history of the Cherokee, native Americans who populated these lands long before the white settlers arrived, is captured in this modern museum. Displays of arrowheads, pottery, and clothing are accompanied by audio and video terminals showing and telling of Cherokee history and myth. It's fun to listen to the Cherokee legends and the sound of the Cherokee language through the cone-shaped earhorns located throughout the museum.

Location On U.S. 441, in the heart of Cherokee, NC

Season
Year-round

Time Allowance
1 - 1.5 hours

Cost Range
$3.50 Adults - $1.50 Children

Bring Along questions, extra money for the gift shop.

Note: Combining a trip to this museum with a visit to the Oconaluftee Indian Village (p. 33) or the outdoor drama, *Unto These Hills* (p. 34), makes for a complete historical outing.

Franklin Gem and Mineral Museum

Located in the old Franklin jail house, this is not your typical mineral museum. As you go from jail cell to jail cell, you'll encounter every rock imaginable as well as an assortment of ancient sea shells and Indian artifacts. There's one room where, in total darkness, you can see how black lights cause different minerals found in an assortment of rocks to glow in iridescent greens, yellows, blues, and reds. You'll think you've just stepped into a science fiction movie!

Location

On Main Street, downtown in Franklin, NC. Phone 704/369-7831.

Season

Year round: 10 a.m. - 4 p.m. (Sundays 1 p.m. - 4 p.m.)

Time Allowance

1 hour

Cost Range

Free

Bring Along

camera, notepad for recording any information, questions.

Note: This is a must if you plan a visit to any of the surrounding gem mines (p. 32). You can learn more about what you found or what to look for before you go.

Folk Art Center

Don't leave this out if you find yourself in the Asheville area. It's a craft museum and shop representing over 200 guild members, but most interesting of all are the various crafters always at work in the front lobby. Depending on the day, you might see brooms being made, pottery being thrown, or sheep being shorn. The crafter may even let you have a go at it yourself. There's a World *Gee Haw Whimmy Diddle* Competition held in early August. If you don't know what a *Gee Haw Whimmy Diddle* is, a trip to the Folk Art Center holds the answer.

Location

Milepost 382 on the Blue Ridge Parkway, one-half mile north of U.S. 70, just east of Asheville, NC. Phone 704/298-7928.

Season
Year-round

Time Allowance
1/2 - 1 hour

Cost Range
Free

Bring Along
camera, questions, extra money for the craft store.

Note: This is a great stop on the way to Craggy Gardens (p. 59) or the WNC Nature Center (p. 44).

Cradle of Forestry

This is the birthplace of modern forestry in America. Here you'll find a visitor center with short movies and an exibit room depicting the advancement of forestry practices in our country. Fun for all is the special childrens area where kids can learn about conservation through the use of puzzles and puppets or by acting out a short play. Outside, two mile-long foot trails lead you back to the turn of the century. You'll see and talk to loggers, blacksmiths, and a various assortment of crafters as you hike along in the forest.

Location   Close to the Blue Ridge Parkway on U.S. 276 north of Brevard, NC in the Pisgah National Forest. Phone 704/877-3130

Season
May - October

Time Allowance
1 - 2 hours

Cost Range
Adults: $2 - Children & Seniors $1

Bring Along   camera, questions, walking shoes, sun protection.

Note: Sliding Rock (p. 19) and the State Trout Hatchery (p. 46) are just down the road. The Blue Ridge Parkway itself (p. 49) has numerous hiking trails and picnic areas.

Watersports

8

Whitewater Rafting

Great fun for children of all ages. Numerous outfitters on several rivers in the area provide rental equipment and guided trips. You'll crash and splash down a boulder-strewn river and soon find it's the perfect way to cool off on a hot summer day. These are the trips many folks use as the centerpiece for their entire vacation.

Locations The **Nantahala River** between Bryson City, NC and Topton, NC on U.S. 74. The **Tuckaseigee River** between Dillsboro, NC and Whittier, NC on U.S. 74.

Season
April - October

Time Allowance
Half-day

Cost Range
Rentals: $5 - $15 per person
Guided trips: $18 - $24 per person
Prices vary between individual outfitters, age, group size and time of year.

Bring Along change of clothes, towel, t-shirt, bathing suit or swim trunks, old shoes you don't mind getting wet, water proof camera, snacks or a picnic for after the trip.

Note: Children must weigh a minimum of 60 pounds to raft on the Nantahala and 40 pounds to raft or tube on the Tuckaseigee. See Appendix for a list of outfitters.

9

River Duckies

You've been whitewater rafting before and you're ready for something a little more challenging. Or maybe you'd like a little separation from the rest of the group. *Voilá*— bring on the duckies! These one-and two-person inflatable kayaks are a world of fun. You're in control, with a little help from the whitewater, and the river is yours to explore on your own. If you liked a particular rapid, you can just pick up your duck, walk back up and do it again.

Locations The **Nantahala River** between Bryson City, NC and Topton, NC on U.S. 74. The **Tuckaseigee River** between Dillsboro, NC and Whittier, NC on U.S. 74.

Season
April - October

Time Allowance
Half-day

Cost Range
$15 - $27 per person

Bring Along change of clothes, towel, t-shirt, swim trunks, old shoes you don't mind getting wet, water proof camera, a snack or picnic for after the trip.

Note: Many times people like to rent both duckies *and* rafts for their group and then change out as they go down the river. Remember that the 60 lb. and 40 lb. weight limits on the Nantahala and Tuckaseigee rivers also apply to duckies.

Canoeing

There are many options for canoeing in the area for those who have (or bring) their own canoe. Of course, swiftwater rivers abound, but these are for experienced whitewater canoeists only. If you're looking for some easier to manage fun, try the waters of Lake Fontana bordering the Great Smoky Mountains National Park. The water is warm and it's fun to explore the quiet, hidden coves while looking for wildlife and old abandoned homesites.

Locations
On Fontana launch from the **USFS Tsali Recreation Area** (just north of Almond, NC on NC 28)and the **USFS Cable Cove Recreation Area** (south of Fontana Dam on NC 28).

Season
April - October

Time Allowance
Half - All Day

Cost Range
Free

Bring Along
change of clothes, towel, t-shirt, swim trunks, old shoes you don't mind getting wet, water proof camera, high energy snacks or picnic for the trip, sun protection, adequate life jackets, lake map.

Note: For an exceptionally fun adventure, launch from Cable Cove and paddle across the lake to the old Hazel Creek Community in the Park for a day of exploration. Don't forget to pick up a map of the lake at Fontana Village before you strike out.

Tubing

On a hot summer day, this is one of the best things going! You're sure to cool off as you float lazily along down the creek, bumping into rocks and spinning like a pinball through the shallow rapids. Hook arms and feet and form a tube train to snake your way down, or see who can go the farthest without getting stuck. However you do it, you can be certain of two things—you're going to get wet and you're going to have fun!

Location   The best place for tubing in the Smokies is on Deep Creek just outside Bryson City, NC at Deep Creek Campground, inside the National Park.

Season
June - August

Time Allowance
Half-day

Cost Range
Tubes rent from $2 - $3 per day each.

Bring Along   change of clothes, towel, t-shirt, swim trunks, old shoes you don't mind getting wet, water proof camera, picnic, sun protection.

Note: It's best to rent the tubes with seats for protection from the rocks. Camping, picnicking, hiking, and horseback riding are also all at Deep Creek. If you bring your own tubes, you float for free!

12

Swimming Pools

Want to go for a swim but having trouble finding a suitable spot? Head for the nearest county recreation department swimming pool. These are open to the public and have life guards on duty. They can be a great place to cool off or to work on your strokes.

Locations The **Swain County Recreation Department Pool** (704/488-6159) is on Deep Creek Road just outside Bryson City, NC and the **Jackson County Recreation Department Pool** (704/586-6333) is on Municipal Drive in downtown Sylva, NC.

Season
June - August

Time Allowance
Half-day

Cost Range
75¢ children - $2 adults

Bring Along change of clothes, towel, t-shirt, swim trunks, sun protection, drinks and snacks.

13

Sliding Rock

There's nothing better than a natural waterslide, and none better than Sliding Rock. For half a century kids have enjoyed sliding down this huge rock slab waterfall in the Pisgah National Forest. Just wade out into the stream, sit down and off you go for the ride of your life to the pool below. Wade over to the side, walk up to the top, and away you go again. It's all done under the watchful eye of the lifeguard on the rock above the pool.

Location   Close to the Blue Ridge Parkway on U.S. 276 north of Brevard, NC in the Pisgah National Forest. Signs mark the spot.

Season
June - August

Time Allowance
2 - 3 hours

Cost Range
Free

Bring Along   change of clothes, towel, t-shirt, swim trunks or shorts with sturdy seat fabric, old shoes you don't mind getting wet, camera, picnic, sun protection.

Note: The water is pretty cold so you'll want to plan a picnic or other break from the slide to warm up. Try the Cradle of Forestry (p. 12) just up the road or the Trout Hatchery (p. 46) down the road toward Brevard.

14

Lake Cruises

Lake Fontana is bordered on one side by the Great Smoky Mountains National Park and the other by the Nantahala National Forest. When this manmade lake flooded the valley many years ago, whole communities were lost or abandoned. There's no better way to see the historic town sites at Hazel Creek or the old homeplaces in Cable Cove than by a pontoon boat cruise on the lake. You'll love skimming along on the water with the reflection of the towering mountains always just ahead of you.

Location
Fontana Village Marina on NC 28 near the Tennessee line on the edge of Lake Fontana.

Season
June - October

Time Allowance
2 hours

Cost Range
$7 per person
$14 per person for picnic cruise

Bring Along
sun protection, camera, drinks and snacks, jacket for cooler days.

Note: If you've planned a trip to see the dam (p. 52) this is a great add-on activity. You may want to call ahead for the daily schedule of departures at 704/498-2211.

Outdoor Activities

15

Picnicking

A picnic can be anything from a convenient impromptu stop on a long trip to a planned family outing. The Smokies are full of fantastic picnic areas, and there's always a good one nearby. Remember, a well-planned picnic can include short hikes, cooling off in nearby streams, games, or nature observation. Below are a few favorite locations.

Locations
Craggy Gardens on the Blue Ridge Parkway just north of Asheville, NC; **Heintooga Overlook** on the Blue Ridge Parkway just outside Cherokee, NC; **Cades Cove** in the National Park just south of Townsend, TN; **Deep Creek** in the National Park just outside Bryson City, NC; **Joyce Kilmer** off US 129 north of Robbinsville, NC

Season
April - October

Time Allowance
2 - 4 hours

Cost Range
Free

Bring Along
food, drinks, table cloth, charcoal for grilling, frisbee, balls, camera, swim suit, old shoes for wading, hiking shoes, garbage bags for cleanup.

16

Day Hikes

It used to be that the only way to see the Smokies was on foot. It's still the best way. With over 800 miles of maintained trails inside the National Park and at least 1000 more nearby, there are plenty to choose from. Many hikes that lead to some pretty special places can be done in less than a day and there are numerous books on the subject (see appendix). Below are a few hikes to get you started.

Location

The **Andrews Bald Trail** (4 miles) starts at the Clingmans Dome parking lot. **Alum Cave Bluff Trail** (4.5 miles) leaves from the Alum Cave Bluffs Parking Area 9 miles south of Sugarlands Visitor Center on US 441. The trailhead for the **Grotto Falls Trail** (3 miles) is located on the Roaring Fork Motor Nature Trail (closed in winter), 2 miles from the entrance.

Season
Year-round

Time Allowance
3 - 4 hours

Cost Range
Free

Bring Along

hiking attire, maps & guidebooks, water bottle, camera, binoculars, sunscreen, day pack, sweater, rain gear, some form of water purification.

Note: No matter what the season, mountain weather can be unpredictable. Never assume stream or spring water is drinkable. Be prepared with some form of water purification (tablets, for instance) in case you run out of the water you bring with you.

17

Camping

Camping has long been an American pastime and there's certainly no shortage of campgrounds in the area covered by this book. For the least expensive and most fun camping experience it's best to plan a stay in one of the ten campgrounds in the National Park or one of the three campgrounds located in the Pisgah National Forest near Brevard, NC. Here you can take advantage of the ranger-led walks, campfires, and lectures, and comfort in the fact that true wilderness is only footsteps away.

Locations See Appendix.

Season
April - October

Time Allowance
Overnight to a week

Cost Range
$6 - $11 per site per night

Bring Along camping equipment, water containers
(no hookups at sites).

Note: Reservations are strongly recommended at Elkmont, Smokemont, and Cades Cove (call 1-800-365-CAMP). All other National Park campgrounds operate on a first-come, first-served basis. For a better chance of finding a space, head for the other, less well-known campgrounds (see Appendix).

Biking

Many folks enjoy bringing their bikes on a trip to the Smokies. If you're camping, most of the campgrounds offer level, lightly-motored roads for cruising around. However, the most popular biking spot in the area is the 11-mile loop road at Cades Cove. Closed in the summer to motor vehicles every Saturday from 7 a.m. to 10 a.m., this gently rolling paved road is perfect for cyclists of all ages. You'll get a little exercise, and you'll also be that much closer to trees, birds, flowers and small animals, experiencing the Smokies in a whole new way.

Location
Cades Cove is located on the western side of the National Park just south of Townsend, TN.

Season
Year-round
Rentals: April - October

Time Allowance
2 - 4 hours to complete loop

Cost Range
Free if you supply your own bike.
Rentals at Cades Cove $3 per hour or $15 per day; child seats available.

Bring Along
comfortable biking clothes and shoes, waterbottles, snacks, camera, sun protection, bike helmet, binoculars.

Mountain Biking

In the last decade, off-road bicycling has exploded in the hills of western North Carolina. The most popular area and the best one for children is the trail system at Tsali Recreation Area. Here, where miles of trails border Lake Fontana, riders can choose from designated mountain bike trails that range in length from 4 to 12 miles.

Location   Tsali Recreation Area is located on NC 28, two miles north of Almond, NC.

Season
Year-round

Time Allowance
Half-day

Cost Range
Free (if you bring your own bikes)
Rentals: $15 - $20 half day

Bring Along   biking clothes and shoes, spare tube, tools, helmet, pump, waterbottle, high energy snack, guide book and map.

Note: Any kid's bike with gears will handle the shorter rides. **Carolina Cycle Tours** at 704/488-6737 and **Euchella Mountain Bikes** at 704/488-8835 rent bikes and equipment on a half-day and daily basis.

#20

Backpacking

An overnight backpacking trip into the mountains is educational, adventuresome, and most of all, fun. You don't have to go far before the world changes and you're suddenly in a land ruled by the elements. Beautiful views, waterfalls, plants, and animals seen only by hikers take on a whole new look. Even though children will usually surprise you with their energy, it's best to keep the distances short and the destinations interesting, ending with a waterfall or large meadow. Below are three special hikes.

Locations
Hazel Creek, on the north side of Lake Fontana, is reached only by boat. Hire a ride from Fontana Village or paddle yourself (p. 16). The first camp site is only 3/10 mile from the lake. **Shining Rock Wilderness** contains several excellent trails (p. 57). Atop **Mt. Le Conte,** (the Park's third highest peak) sits a popular rustic lodge (booked far in advance) and a trail shelter. To get to the top, take the **Alum Cave Bluff Trail** (p. 23); it's 5.5 miles with a gain of 3900 feet.

Season
Year-round (best in warmer months)

Time Allowance
Overnight with 2 - 4 hours of hiking each day.

Cost Range
Free

Bring Along
good hiking shoes, comfortable, well-padded light packs with all your gear, camera, water and a means of water purification, guidebooks and maps (see Appendix), back country permit (available free at ranger stations).

Horseback Riding

Most children love horses. That you can count on. For those who have never been on a horse, a short guided trail ride in or near the national park is a wonderful first experience. You'll saddle up, get some instruction, and then head off down the trail, one behind the other, in a regular horse train with your guide leading the way.

Locations
See Appendix for a listing of horse stables in the area.

Season
April - October

Time Allowance
1 - 2 hours

Cost Range
$9 - $12 per hour per person

Bring Along
comfortable riding clothing, sturdy shoes, camera, sun protection.

Note: Most stables also offer half, full and multiday options. These can be quite costly. If you have your own horse, many of the trails in the area are open to horseback riding at no charge.

Classic Attractions

22

Great Smoky Mountains Railway

The whistle blows and it's all aboard for one of the most popular attractions in the Smokies. Planned properly, these excursions can make for a fun morning or afternoon. Bouncing along in the converted rail cars you'll pass through tunnels, over high trestles, and alongside whitewater rivers as bluegrass music, local lore, stories, and legends are piped into your car.

Locations
Dillsboro Depot, Dillsboro, NC and Bryson City Depot, Bryson City, NC. Phone 800/872-4681 or 704/586-8811.

Season
June - October
Weekends only in April and May

Time Allowance
Half-day

Cost Range
Children under 13 yrs: $7 — Adults: $14 - $16

Bring Along
camera, binoculars, sack lunch or snacks, drinks.

Note: Higher-priced options which can include a buffet lunch, a raft trip on the Nantahala River, or a special steam-powered locomotive are also available. If you want an open air car, be sure to call ahead for reservations.

23

Trout Ponds

Tired of fishing and not catching any fish? Ready for some guaranteed success? Head for the nearest trout pond. They'll supply you with everything you need and they'll even clean and prepare your catch. Kids will love reeling in whopper after whopper and you can bet they'll have a whopper of a fish tale to tell afterwards.

Locations
See Appendix for a listing of trout ponds in the area.

Season
April - October

Time Allowance
1 - 2 hours

Cost Range
$2 -$3 per pound, you must keep everything you catch.

Bring Along
your own fishing equipment (it will be provided if you don't have any), camera, ice cooler to bring fish back in.

Note: This is a great activity, especially if you've fished on a stream for a while with no luck or have never ever caught a fish. It's also the most fun and inexpensive way to shop if you want trout for dinner. No licenses are required.

24

Gem Mines

Gem mines abound in the Cowee Valley near Franklin. Years ago the streams in the area were actively mined for rubies and other stones. Today, with a little instruction, you can give it a go yourself. At the mines you start with a bucket or two of mud from a nearby stream and a fabricated mining screen, then take your place along the mine race. Everyone loves this search for hidden treasures because each time there's no telling what you'll find.

Locations
The best mines are located in the Cowee Valley, just off NC 28, five miles north of Franklin, NC (see Appendix for a list of gem mines).

Season
April - October

Time Allowance
2 - 3 hours

Cost Range
$6 to $7 per person (some mines are half-price for kids), plus 50¢ to $1 per bucket of mud.

Bring Along
hats, sunscreen, change of clothes and shoes for the kids (they're bound to get wet), water, snacks.

Note: "Native" mines use only the dirt from the stream. "Enriched" mines provide an almost guranteed find of any range of gems. Try combining this trip with a visit to the Franklin Gem and Mineral Museum (p. 10).

25

Oconaluftee Indian Village

As you enter the gates of this village, you'll be transported back in time over 200 years. A Cherokee Indian guide will explain his heritage as he leads your group to different demonstration areas showing aspects of Cherokee culture, from blowguns to the making of dugout canoes. Everything is very realistic and you'll enjoy asking questions of the various tribal members. The tour ends in the council house where you're brought back to the present with an explanation of Cherokee life as it is today.

Location
Just off US 441 in downtown Cherokee, NC. Phone 704/497-2315.

Season
May 15 - October 25
Open 9 a.m. to 5:30 p.m.

Time Allowance
1 hour
Tours leave every 15 minutes.

Cost Range
Adults: $8 -- Children (6 - 13): $4

Bring Along
camera, walking shoes, questions.

Note: You will want to make this a part of your day in Cherokee and might combine it with a trip to the Museum of the Cherokee Indian (p. 9) and the outdoor drama *Unto These Hills* (p. 34).

Unto These Hills

A history of the Cherokee Indian is portrayed in this popular outdoor performance. You'll see how the lives of this peace-loving people changed from the time of Spanish exploration in 1540 to its near-extinction during the infamous "trail of tears" several hundred years later. The performance includes lots of sound and action, from the booms of pioneer muskets to the magic of the tribal dancers.

Location
Just off US 441 in downtown Cherokee, NC. Phone 704/497-2111.

Season
Nightly except Sunday, mid-June through late August

Time Allowance
2 hours

Cost Range
Adults: $8 -- Children: $5 (General Admission)
All Ages: $10 (Reserved Seating)

Bring Along
warm clothes, rain jackets or umbrella, stadium blanket, camera, binoculars

Note: The show starts at 8:45 pm until the last weekend in July and then at 8:30 pm through August. The seats are not covered so if it starts to rain, you'll need rain gear. Night time in the mountains can be chilly, so come prepared. You'll want to arrive early for two reasons: good seats (general admission) and the cast's performance of folk songs 1/2 hour before the show.

#27

Appalachian Trail

Stretching over 2000 miles and spanning 14 states, this hiking trail passes right through the heart of the Smokies. Quite a few folks hike the entire length of the AT each year. These rugged individuals are known as "through hikers." If you have only a few hours (instead of several months), a shorter hike on the trail can be very rewarding. Access to several good walks on the AT can be found as it passes through this area. It's well marked with signs and white blazes. Don't be surprised when the kids come away saying that they, too, hiked the Appalachian Trail.

Locations **Newfound Gap** on US 441 in the National Park. **Clingman's Dome** off US 441 from Newfound Gap. **Fontana Dam** on NC 28 at the southwestern corner of the Park (the trail crosses the dam!). **Nantahala Outdoor Center** on US 74, 15 miles west of Bryson City, NC. Get directions in the outfitters store.

Season
Year-round

Time Allowance
15 minutes - 2 hours

Cost Range
Free

Bring Along comfortable walking clothing, sturdy shoes, camera, sun protection, water.

Note: This can be a good leg stretcher activity on some of the auto tour excursions (pps. 52 & 56) or after a raft trip on the Nantahala River (p. 14).

Special Events

Throughout the season there are many special events worth visiting if you're in the area when they occur. You can count on finding something going on Memorial Day, the Fourth of July, or Labor Day in just about any of the local communities. A lot of the fun is "discovering" an event on your own. Below is a partial list just to get you started with space left for you to fill in your own discoveries. Keep a keen eye to the newspapers and a listening ear to the radio. You'll soon be venturing out to who knows where.

Event	Location	Dates
Belle Chere	Asheville, NC	August
WCU Mountain Heritage Day	Cullowhee, NC	September
Fireman's Day	Bryson City, NC	Early September
Dillsboro's Luminaire	Dillsboro, NC	Early December
Chili Cookoff	Bryson City, NC	Late October

Time Allowance
Half-day

Cost Range
Most are free

Bring Along
camera, walking shoes, money for crafts, food, balloons, etc., picnic.

Back to Nature

Quiet Walkways

Scattered throughout the Great Smoky Mountains National Park and adjacent to the major roads, these walkways provide instant escape into the edge of the wilderness. They are hardly ever more than a half of a mile in length, so you can expect them not to be too difficult. If you find yourself in slow, bumper-to-bumper traffic (which can occur easily in peak season) or even if there is not another car on the road, and you spot the familiar "Quiet Walkway" sign, pull over and give everyone a break. You'll be glad you did.

Locations There are numerous quiet walkways located on all the paved roads inside the National Park. Look for the signs.

Season
Year-round

Time Allowance
10 minutes to 1/2 hour

Cost Range
Free

Bring Along camera, walking shoes, binoculars.

Note: You really don't *need* anything special for the walk, not even walking shoes. The idea is to take a break from the mechanical world of autos and noise and experience the quiet natural surroundings first-hand.

Nature Trails

Want to see a lichen close up, or learn how to tell a Hemlock from a Spruce? Maybe you'd like to walk through a heath bald. You can do this and plenty more on one of the self-guiding nature trails. There are a total of 11 within the Great Smoky Mountains National Park. Each has its own guide you can pick up at the start. As you walk along the leaflet points out special things to look for while giving you descriptions and a history of the area. Walks range from 1/3 to 5 miles with the majority under a mile in length.

Locations Trails are located at a number of the camp-grounds as well as Sugarlands Visitor Center and off the major roads. A booklet listing all trails is available in Park visitor centers.

Season
Year-round

Time Allowance
1 - 1.5 hours

Cost Range
Free

Bring Along hiking shoes, water bottle, camera, binoculars, clothes for the season plus an extra layer, rain gear.

Note: If you plan to do the Alum Cave Nature Trail, plan at least a half day and take food and water. Weather can be unpredictable in the Park so whenever you are out for more than an hour take along an extra layer, plus rain gear, just in case.

Ranger-Led Activities

No one knows the Smokies better than the National Park Rangers, so why choose any one else to learn from? Almost every day during the season somewhere in the Park there will be a ranger-led activity. It could be a nature hike, a cemetery walk, a hayride, a story telling session, or a hike in the dark. You might find yourself practicing bird calls or sitting wide-eyed around a campfire. No matter what you choose, you can bet it will be fun and informative.

Locations   The best way to find out what and where activities are being held is to pick up a free copy of the *Smokies Guide* at a ranger station or check the bulletin board at a Park campground.

Season
April - October

Time Allowance
1/2 hour - Half-day

Cost Range
Free

Bring Along   camera, walking shoes, binoculars, extra layer of clothes, rain jacket, water bottle.

#32

Wildlife Observation

There's nothing more exciting than spotting a bear. Just the sight of one in Cades Cove has been known to cause a "bear jam" that would rival gridlock in any city. Bears are wild animals, just like the deer, the foxes, the ground hogs, the grouse, the pileated wood-peckers and the seldom seen red wolf. You can see these and plenty more here in the Smokies. What's fun is to keep a running log of the different animals you see, how many, and where. Who can spot the largest, most unusual, and most colorful animals?

Locations Almost anywhere, but the best places are the fields at Cades Cove and Cataloochee in the Park and along the Blue Ridge Parkway.

Season
Year-round

Time Allowance
As long as you like

Cost Range
Free

Bring Along camera, binoculars, notebook or log, field guides for birds, mammals, amphibians, etc.

Note: The best time of day to spot larger mammals is just after sunrise and just before sunset when they come out to feed. An excellent way to escape the potential "bear jams" at Cades Cove is to go by bike on Saturday morning (see p. 25). **Remember: never feed any bear or other wild animal.**

Leaf Lookin'

In appreciation of all the many visits to the Smokies each year, the trees put on a special show of their own. They know that as the weather turns colder people will no longer come to admire them and relax under their shade. They use the last bit of energy they have to turn their leaves brilliant shades of red, orange, yellow, and gold. This, of course, brings the people back by the thousands. Finally, when the trees are tired, they drop their leaves in a crackly carpet of brown. Then the people leave and the trees stand bare and proud through the cold winter.

Locations   Leaves in the higher elevations change color first, so head for the Blue Ridge Parkway, Clingman's Dome, or Newfound Gap. In the peak of the season, anywhere is good.

Season
Late September - October

Time Allowance
1/2 hour - All day

Cost Range
Free

Bring Along   camera, binoculars, sweater, rain jacket, leaf or fall color guide (see Appendix).

Note: Mix leaf lookin' with other activities such as: day hikes (page 23), car travel (pps. 48 & 54), the natural wonders (pps. 56 & 60), a lake cruise (p. 20) or a train ride (p. 30) to round out a trip.

#34

Spotting Wildflowers

With over 1500 flowering plants, the Smokies is a regular paradise on earth. From mid-April through October the forests and fields are alive with flowers. First come the snowy white dogwoods, multi-colored trilliums, violets, lady's slippers, and jack-in-the-pulpits. Next to emerge, in May and June, come the white or pink mountain laurel and orange flame azaleas. In late June and July you'll see the famous catawba and rosebay rhododendron. Finally, in September and October, look for goldenrod, ironweed, and asters scattered in the fields. In between all these you'll spot hundreds more.

Locations

You're bound to spot wildflowers just about anywhere in the Smokies. A great information source for local hotspots is the free *Smokies Guide* found in Park visitor centers.

Season
Mid-April - October

Time Allowance
As long as you like

Cost Range
Free

Bring Along
camera, binoculars, notebook or log, field guides for wildflowers (see Appendix).

Note: One of the most beautiful displays of rhododendron can be found at Craggy Gardens, a great spot for a picnic (p. 59).
Remember: It's illegal to pick or remove flowers or other plants from the Park.

35

Western North Carolina Nature Center

Turtles, frogs, snakes, spiders, turkeys, owls, eagles, deer, foxes, otters, cougars, wolves, and bears. They're all native to these mountains (or once were) and you may have seen some in the wild already. At the Nature Center you can see them live and close up while you learn more about their natural environment. You'll find an observation room with microscopes, a working beehive, and plenty of rocks, skulls, and bones to pick up and feel. You can even mine for mealworms. The chickens, goats, sheep, and peacocks in the petting area are hard to resist. Which animal will you like the best?

Location   On Gashes Creek Road near the eastern city limits of Asheville, NC. Follow the directional signs from I-40, I-240, US 70, or NC 81. Phone 704/298-5600.

Season
Summer: 10 - 5, Mon. through Sat.; 1 - 5 Sun.
Winter: 10 - 5, Tue. through Sat.; 1 - 5 Sun.; closed Mon.

Time Allowance
1.5 - 4 hours

Cost Range
Adults: $2.50 -- Children: $1.50

Bring Along   camera, walking shoes.

Note: Just outside the Nature Center is an old-time amusement park with a number of fun and inexpensive rides that are hard to pass up. There's also a picnic area on the grounds. You might combine this trip with a Craggy Gardens excursion (p. 59) or a visit to the Folk Art Center (p. 11).

Berry Pickin'

Wild blueberry cobbler, fresh blackberries on cereal, just-turned homemade huckleberry ice cream. Yum. With a little effort these scrumptious, palate-pleasing delicacies can be yours. In fact, they are just a hand's reach away. Berries abound in the Smokies in summertime and there's nothing more rewarding than picking a pail or two for the table.

Locations

The best place to pick wild blueberies is along the Blue Ridge Parkway and at the entrance to Shining Rock Wilderness (p. 57). Blackberries are found in fields in the valleys, in timbercuts, and alongside roadways.

Season
Blackberries: late June & July
Huckleberries and blueberries: late August

Time Allowance
As long as you like.

Cost Range
Free

Bring Along

picking pails (milk jugs cut off at the top and attached to your belt at the waist work well), water, sun protection, snacks, picnic.

Note: Always be sure to ask permission before venturing onto private land.

Trout Hatchery

The streams in the Smokies teem with trout and the reason why can be found at the Pisgah Trout Hatchery. At this state-supported hatchery, trout are raised in long, concrete, simulated streams until they reach an appropriate size. They are then deposited in many of western North Carolina's streams and rivers where anglers tempt them with hand-tied flies. One fun thing to do is buy a handful of feed from the gum ball machines at the hatchery and toss it to the fish. The water is crystal clear and you'll see hundreds of trout wrestling for the food. Inside the headquarters there's a small trout museum.

Location Just off US 276, north of Brevard, NC in the Pisgah National Forest

Season
Year-round

Time Allowance
1/2 - 1 hour

Cost Range
Free

Bring Along camera, change for the gumball/fish feed machine.

Note: This is a great side trip if you are spending the day at Sliding Rock (p. 19), visiting the Cradle of Forestry (p. 12) or touring the Blue Ridge Parkway (p. 49).

Car Travel

Cades Cove

This is the most popular drive in the Smokies and maybe in the East. It's no wonder— Cades Cove is a remarkably beautiful place. No matter what time of year you choose to visit, you can count on seeing picture-book scenes. Old homesteads, churches, a grist mill, and miles of rolling green meadows are surrounded by towering mountains. This one-way loop road is also the best place in the Park to view wildlife from your car.

Location
In the northwest corner of the Great Smoky Mountains National Park near Townsend, TN

Season
Year-round

Time Allowance
Driving time 1 hour

Cost Range
Free

Bring Along
camera, binoculars, picnic, walking shoes, field guides for plants, animals, and flowers. Be sure to pick up a tour pamphlet at the start.

Note: During peak season (July, August, October) there can be quite a lot of traffic on this road. Try touring early morning or late afternoon to miss the crowds. Dawn and twilight are also the best times to spot wildlife (p. 41). Don't miss the visitor center halfway around the loop (p. 7).

39

Blue Ridge Parkway

Connecting the Shenandoah and Great Smoky Mountains National Parks, this 470-mile winding ribbon of asphalt is certainly a national treasure. The southern end of the Parkway traverses very rugged terrain. There are long, dark tunnels, cliffs, and waterfalls around every bend. As you drive along, you'll see spectacular views from numerous overlooks and picnic areas. In fact, you'll sometimes be so high up, you can reach out your window and wash your hands in the clouds.

Location The southern entrance to the Blue Ridge Parkway is just north of Cherokee, NC off US 441. Other convenient entrances are off US 74 just west of Waynesville, NC and off I-26 or I-40 near Asheville, NC.

Season
Some sections closed in winter

Time Allowance
As long as you like

Cost Range
Free

Bring Along camera, binoculars, picnic, a full tank of gas (stations are few and far between), walking shoes.

Note: A drive on the Parkway is a great trip in itself, or a superb way to get to many of the other destinations listed in this book. On rainy days the Parkway can be smothered in dense fog.

Foothills Parkway

This drive is only 17 miles long and a junior version of the Blue Ridge Parkway. Its most noted feature is Look Rock and its observation tower. From the tower on Look Rock you can see the Smokies in all their splendor in one direction and the Tennessee Valley, the town of Maryville, and the Cumberland Plateau in the other.

Location Entrances are on US 321 north of Townsend, TN and on US 129 at the northwestern corner of the Great Smoky Mountains National Park.

Season
Year-round

Time Allowance
1 hour

Cost Range
Free

Bring Along camera, binoculars, walking shoes.

Note: This is a good add-on if you're making a trip to Fontana Dam (p. 52) or if you're touring the Parson Branch Road (p. 54). There is another 6-mile eastern stretch of the Foothills Parkway that makes for a scenic shortcut from Cosby, TN to I-40.

41

The Road To Nowhere

Have you ever wanted to go to nowhere? Now's your opportunity because "nowhere" is right here in the Smokies. When the National Park was established in the early 1940's, whole communities were swallowed up by the Park's boundaries. This road was intended to provide a route to old grave sites and homesteads that were made inaccessible by Lake Fontana. At the end of the road is a tunnel and on the other side of the tunnel is nowhere—the road was never completed. Vehicles are not allowed in the tunnel, but people are. It's a long, dark, spooky, and fun walk to the other side.

Location   From Bryson City, NC take Everett Street north, out of town. After 2.5 miles you'll see a sign on the left that says "Welcome to a road to nowhere...Broken Promise...1943 - ?".

Season
Year-round

Time Allowance
1.5 - 2 hours

Cost Range
Free

Bring Along   camera, binoculars, walking shoes.

Note: The official name of this road is Lakeview Drive. Along the road are a number of quiet walkways. You may want to combine this outing with a train ride (p. 30) or creek tubing (p. 17).

Fontana Dam

This is the highest dam east of the Rockies and it is a sight to behold. Standing at the bottom looking up can be pretty scary when you think about all the water behind it, but don't worry, it's very safe. Tours are given inside the dam and there is an observation tower on top. As you walk or drive across the top be sure to look for the white trail blazes painted on the concrete that mark the route of the Appalachian Trail as it crosses here on its way north to Maine.

Location
At the southwest corner of the Great Smoky Mountains National Park on NC 28 at the end of Lake Fontana

Season
Year-round
(Visitor building staffed May - October)

Time Allowance
1- 2 hours

Cost Range
Free

Bring Along
camera, binoculars, picnic

Note: Consider taking a lake cruise while you're at the dam (p. 20). Every year on the 4th of July, Fontana Village puts on a fireworks display. There is no better place from which to watch than the top of the dam.

43

Roaring Fork Motor Nature Trail

This five-mile auto tour, located just minutes from the bustling tourist town of Gatlinburg and inside the Great Smoky Mountains National Park, is both a nature and historical trail. You'll be amazed at the contrast you experience on leaving the city and heading into the Park. From the pamphlet you pick up at the start you'll learn about the different types of forests you pass through as well as the climate and geology of the area. Roaring Fork was once a mountain community and there are several old homesteads still in the area. This is a wonderful tour and a quick get-away from the rush in town.

Location   Just outside Gatlinburg, TN in the National Park. From 441 in Gatlinburg, turn south onto Airport Road at light #8. Drive 1/2 mile and then turn right again on Cherokee Orchard Road. It's 3.2 miles to the entrance.

Season
Closed in winter

Time Allowance
1 hour

Cost Range
Free

Bring Along   camera, binoculars, field guides.

Note: This road is closed to busses, motor homes, and vehicles towing trailers. You might want to combine this drive with a hike to Grotto Falls (p. 23).

Backroads

Throughout the Smokies are a variety of back roads, traveled by few, that take you through wonderful places. The interesting thing is that almost no one knows they exist and when you find one on your own, it's a real discovery. Inside the National Park there are three such roads: Parson Branch Road, Rich Mountain Road, and Round Bottom Road. Each is unique in itself. After you've given these a try, find some of your own.

Locations

Parson Branch Road originates off the Cades Cove Loop Road just past the vistor center and ends on US 129 next to the TN/NC state line. **Rich Mountain Road** originates off the Cades Cove Loop Road several miles before you reach the visitor center and ends on US 321 near Townsend, TN. **Round Bottom Road** originates at the Heintooga Overlook/Balsam Mountain picnic area on the Blue Ridge Parkway and ends in Cherokee, NC.

Season

May - October (roads closed in winter)

Time Allowance

Allow approximately 1 hour each

Cost Range

Free

Bring Along

camera, binoculars, map.

Note: These roads are not suitable for motor homes or cars pulling trailers.

Natural Wonders

#45

Clingman's Dome

This is the highest peak in the Smokies and the second highest east of the Mississippi. It stands at 6,642 feet above sea level. On the summit is an observation tower that takes you up another 45 feet. The climb to the top is up a sloping paved walkway. From here, on a clear day, you get an unobstructed 360° view.

Location
From Newfound Gap take the Clingman's Dome spur road 7 miles to the top

Season
Road may be closed in winter

Time Allowance
1/2 - 1 hour

Cost Range
Free

Bring Along
camera, binoculars, warm clothes (it can be cold up top), walking shoes.

Note: There are several good hiking trails to be found here. Andrews Bald (p. 23) and the Spruce-Fir Nature Trail are two of them.

Shining Rock

The neat thing about this national wilderness area is that the only way to get to it is to walk in. There are a number of trails leading into the area, but the best one is the Ivestor Gap Trail. It's 2 miles one way to the wilderness boundary and even though it's all above 5000 feet, the trail is relatively level. The "shining rock" is actually a large outcropping of white quartz located several miles into the area. If you look closely, you can spot it sparkling in the sunlight on a ridge off to the northeast of the trailhead parking lot.

Location   Near Waynesville, NC. At milepost 420 on the Blue Ridge Parkway turn onto Forest Service Road 816. The Ivestor Gap Trailhead is at the end of this road.

Season
Year-round

Time Allowance
Half-day

Cost Range
Free

Bring Along   camera, binoculars, map, hiking shoes, water, high energy snacks, sun protection, extra layers, rain gear.

Note: This is the place to go berry picking in late August (p. 45). A good round-trip hike is to return from Ivestor Gap on the Art Loeb Trail. It follows the high ridgeline and comes out just above the parking area. Shining Rock makes for a good stop while touring the Blue Ridge Parkway (p. 49).

47

Joyce Kilmer

You'll find some of the biggest trees in the eastern United States in this national wilderness area. A two-mile loop trail winds its way through a virgin forest where trees reach over twenty feet in circumference. If you have enough people, see how many it takes to link hands and stretch around the largest of the trees. You'll be amazed as you find yourself dwarfed by one after another of these monsters.

Location Take US 129 north out of Robbinsville, NC and follow the signs to Joyce Kilmer Wilderness Area

Season
Year-round

Time Allowance
1 hour

Cost Range
Free

Bring Along camera, binoculars, walking shoes, field guide to trees and plants.

Note: Be sure to drive up the 4.5-mile observation point road where there's a great view of Lake Santeetla from a wooden platform. Also, this isn't very far from Fontana Dam (p. 52) or the west end of Parson Branch Road (p. 54) if you're looking for a nice complement to one of those trips.

Craggy Gardens

This amazing heath bald covered with rhododendron sits high above Asheville and right on the Blue Ridge Parkway. In mid-June it's a blaze of pink and one of the prettiest sights around. From the parking area, on the other side of the tunnel from the visitor center, there's a short trail to the top of Craggy Pinnacle that you won't want to miss. This trail leads through a magical grove of catawba rhododendron to a stone observation deck that overlooks the gardens, the Blue Ridge Parkway, and the rest of the Smokies.

Location   At milepost 364 on the Blue Ridge Parkway 18 miles east of Asheville, NC

Season
Year-round

Time Allowance
1 hour

Cost Range
Free

Bring Along   camera, binoculars, hiking shoes, sun protection, extra layers, rain gear, picnic.

Note: This is a great place for a picnic (p. 22). It's also a nice excursion if you find yourself in Asheville at the WNC Nature Center (p. 44) or the Folk Art Center (p. 11).

49

Waterfalls

No one knows how many waterfalls there are in the Smokies; they're just too numerous to count. There are big ones, little ones, tall ones, and short ones. There are those found way back in the wilderness and those that cascade almost right on top of the road. They can be spectacular to look at and they seem to multiply in number after a heavy rain. It's fun to stand at the bottom of larger waterfalls and feel the cool mist caused by the force of the water blowing across your face, and standing next to any size falls is like entering an air conditioned room. Below are several good ones to look for.

Locations **Laurel Falls** on US 321 in the Park, 3.6 miles west of Sugarlands Visitor Center. **Grotto Falls** (p. 23). **Looking Glass Falls** on US 276, just south of Sliding Rock (p. 19).

Season
Year-round

Time Allowance
As long as you like

Cost Range
Free

Bring Along camera, binoculars, walking shoes,
maps and guidebooks (see Appendix).

Note: Climbing on or near waterfalls is very dangerous. Don't do it!

Appendix

Sample Itineraries

Many of the activities in this book are located in close proximity to one another. A well-planned day can include a number of things that not only complement each other but help reduce time lost by driving around. Below are several itineraries you can try for yourself. They should also give you ideas on how you might use this book to plan your own daily outings.

• A History Lesson in Cherokee

Cherokee, NC is in the heart of the Qualla Cherokee Indian Reservation and on the edge of the Great Smoky Mountains National Park. You'll notice as soon as you arrive that there are a lot of attractions that will tempt your purse. Running the gauntlet of tourist shops can be quite overwhelming. However, there are several particularly worthwhile stops. Start with a visit to the **Museum of the Cherokee Indian** (p. 9) then head up the road to the **Oconaluftee Indian Village** (p. 33). Depending on what time you start, this can fill a morning or afternoon. If you've still got the energy and the finances, stick around for the outdoor drama *Unto These Hills* (p. 34) starting around 8 P.M.

• A Rainy Day

It rains quite often in the Smokies and a rainy day does not mean there's nothing to do. Head for the **Franklin Gem and Mineral Museum** (p. 10). It doesn't take long, you learn a lot, and it may stop raining while you're there. Don't worry if it doesn't. The perfect complement to the museum is a trip to the **Gem Mines** (p. 32). Many have covered flumes to keep off both the rain and the sun. Another alternative when the rain sets in is to go nowhere at all. **The Road to Nowhere,** that is (p. 51). You're not likely to get too wet walking through the old tunnel.

• A Day in Pisgah

The Pisgah National Forest near Brevard, NC has long been a favorite destination for families with children. It's no wonder, with all there is to do. Start the day with a visit to the **Trout Hatchery** (p. 46). Seeing the hordes of fish is fun and it will give the sun time to warm things up a bit before you head up the road to **Sliding Rock** (p. 19). Be sure to stop at **Looking Glass Falls** on the way. After you're sufficiently cooled off, take time out for a picnic and a visit to the **Cradle of Forestry** (p. 12). There's probably still time for a few more slides down the rock before calling it a day. You can get to and from Pisgah via the **Blue Ridge Parkway** (p. 49).

Places to Stay That Cater to Children

• Nantahala Village Resort
9400 Highway 19W
Bryson City, NC 28713
704/488-2826 or (outside NC) 800/438-1507
Open mid-March through December. Lodge, cabins, restaurant, pool, rafting, horseback riding, and mountain biking—very good and reasonably priced. Full-time childrens activities director in summer. Located in the Nantahala Gorge.

• Freeman's Motel and Cabins
P.O. Box 100
Almond, NC 28702
704/488-2737
Open year-round. Cabins, rooms and pool. Close to Lake Fontana. Family-oriented.

- **New Wonderland Hotel**
  3889 Wonderland Way
  Sevierville, TN 37862
  615/436-5490
  Open mid-March through December. Lodge, cabins, hiking, and horseback riding. A stone's throw from the Great Smoky Mountains National Park. This is the new version of the 80-year-old Wonderland Hotel formerly located at Elkmont in the Park.

Public Campgrounds

Unless a phone number is listed, sites are available on a first-come, first-served basis.

- **Abrams Creek**
  16 sites, $6 per night.
  In the northwest corner of the Park, near Townsend, TN.

- **Balsam Mountain**
  45 sites, $8 per night.
  Just off the Blue Ridge Parkway, above Cherokee, NC.

- **Big Creek**
  12 sites, $6 per night. Walk-in sites only.
  In Tennessee in the northeast corner of the Park, near I-40.

- **Cades Cove**
  161 sites, $11 per night. Call 800/365-CAMP.
  Close to Townsend, TN.

- **Cataloochee**
  27 sites, $6 per night.
  Near Maggie Valley, NC.

- **Cosby**
  174 sites, $8 per night (rarely full)
  Near Cosby, TN.

- **Deep Creek**
    122 sites, $8 per night.
    Near Bryson City, NC.

- **Elkmont**
    218 sites, $11 per night. Call 800/365-CAMP.
    Just off US 321 between Gatlinburg, TN and Townsend, TN.

- **Look Rock**
    92 sites, $8 per night (rarely fills).
    On the Foothills Parkway.

- **Smokemont**
    140 sites, $11 per night. Call 800/365-CAMP.
    Closest to Cherokee.

- **Davidson River Campground**
    $8 per night.
    In the Pisgah National Forest near Brevard, NC.

- **North Mills River Campground**
    $8 per night.
    In the Pisgah National Forest, west of Hendersonville, NC.

- **Mount Pisgah Campground**
    140 sites. Call 704/235-8228
    On the Blue Ridge Parkway, just west of Asheville, NC.

Whitewater Outfitters

- **Nantahala Outdoor Center**
  13077 Highway 19W
  Bryson City, NC 28713
  800/232-7238 or 704/488-6900
  Located on the Nantahala River. Guided raft trips and raft, ducky, and canoe rentals. Kayak school. 3 restaurants. Outfitters store. Daycare facility.

- **Wildwater, Ltd.**
  Highway 19W
  Bryson City, NC 28713
  704/488-2384
  Guided raft trips on the Nantahala River.

- **Rolling Thunder River Company**
  P.O. Box 88
  Almond, NC 28702
  800/344-5838 or 704/488-2030
  Guided raft trips and raft, ducky and canoe rentals on the Nantahala River.

- **Great Smokies Rafting Company**
  Highway 19W
  Bryson City, NC 28713
  800/277- 6302 or 704/488-6302
  Located at Nantahala Village Resort. Guided raft trips and raft and ducky rentals on the Nantahala River.

- **Tuckaseegee Outfitters**
  Box 1719
  Cullowhee, NC 28723
  704/586-5050
  Guided raft trips and raft, ducky, canoe, and tube rentals on the Tuckaseegee River.

Horse Stables

- **Cades Cove Riding Stable**
  615/448-6286
  Located in Cades Cove in the National Park.

- **Deep Creek Riding Stable**
  Located at Deep Creek Campground in the National Park.

- **McCarter's Riding Stable**
  615/436-5354
  Located near Sugarlands Visitor Center in the National Park.

- **Smokemont Riding Stable**
  704/497-2373
  Located at Smokemont Campground near Cherokee in the National Park.

- **Nantahala Village Riding Stable**
  704/488-9649
  Located at Nantahala Village Resort in the Nantahala Gorge.

Cowee Valley Gem Mines

- **Jones Ruby Mine**
  Ruby Mine Road, Franklin, NC. Phone 704/524-5946
  Native and other North Carolina stones.

- **Sheffield Mine**
  Leatherman Gap Road, Franklin, NC. Phone 704/369-8383
  Native stones only.

- **The Old Cardinal Gem Mine**
  Mason Branch Road, Franklin, NC. Phone 704/369-7534
  Native and enriched stones.

Trout Ponds

- **Cherokee Trout Farm**
  Big Cove Road
  Cherokee, NC
  704/497-9227

- **Guffey's Trout Pond**
  Highway 19W
  Topton, NC
  704/321-3587

- **Ward's Trout Pond**
  Highway 74/441
  Whittier, NC
  704/497-7533

- **Great Smoky Mountain Trout**
  Bunches Creek
  Cherokee, NC
  704/497-5507

- **Soco Gap Trout Ponds**
  Hwy. 19W
  Maggie Valley, NC
  704/926-3635

Area Guides

- *Time Well Spent, Family Hiking in the Smokies* by Hal Hubs, Charles Maynard, and David Morris

- *Great Walks, The Great Smokies* by Robert Gillmore

- *OFF THE BEATEN TRACK, A Guide to Mountain Biking in Western North Carolina (Vols. I & II)* by Jim Parham

- *Leaflookers Guide to Splendor in the Mountains* by John Powell and Moody Barrick

- *Great Smoky Mountains Wildflowers* by Carlos Campbell, William Hutson, and Aaron Sharpe.

49
Fun & Inexpensive

THINGS
TO DO IN THE
SMOKIES
With Children

by Jim Parham

Also by Jim Parham:

OFF THE BEATEN TRACK—
A Guide to Mountain Biking in
Western North Carolina

OFF THE BEATEN TRACK—
A Guide to Mountain Biking
in Western North Carolina;
Volume II: Pisgah National Forest

Copyright © 1993 by Jim Parham

All rights reserved. *No part of this book may be reproduced without the express written consent of the publisher, except in the case of brief excerpts in critical reviews and articles.*

WMC Publishing, P.O. Box 158, Almond, NC 28702

ISBN 0-9631861-2-4 $5.95

Cover design and illustrations by Frank Lee

A great deal of information is contained in this book and every effort has been made to provide this information as accurately as possible. However, prices, locations and other information are subject to change with time.

Printed on recycled paper.